The Hudson Letter

The
HUDSON
Letter
Derek Mahon

Wake Forest University Press

Wake Forest

University Press.

This book is for sale

only in North America.

Poems copyright Derek Mahon

All rights reserved.

For permission, required

to reprint or broadcast more

than several lines, write to:

Wake Forest University Press,

Post Office Box 7333

Winston-Salem, NC 27109

Set in Garamond

Printed by Thomson Shore

LC Card No. 95-62043

ISBN 0-916390-70-5 (paperback)

ISBN 0-916390-71-3 (clothbound)

Contents

Noon at St. Michael's

Nurses and nuns —
their sails whiter than those
of the yachts in the bay, they come and go
on winged feet, most of them, or in 'sensible' shoes.
July, and I should be climbing among stones
or diving, but for broken bones,
from the rocks below.

I try to read
a new novel set aside;
but a sword-swift pain
in the left shoulder-blade, the result
of a tumble in Sheridan Square, makes reading difficult.
Writing you can do in your head.
It starts to rain

on the sea,
suddenly dark, the pier,
the gardens and the church spires of Dun Laoghaire.
You would think it was suddenly October
as smoke flaps, the yachts tack violently
and those caught in the downpour
run for cover.

But in a few
minutes the sun shines again,
the leaves and hedges glisten as if with dew
in that fragrant freshness after rain
when the world seems made anew
before confusion, before pain;
and I think of you,

a funny-face
but solemn, with the sharpest mind I know,
a thoughtful creature of unconscious grace
bent to your books in the sun or driving down
to New York for an evening on the town.
Doors open wherever you go
in that furious place;

for you are the light
rising on lost islands, the *spéir-bhean*
the old poets saw gleam in the morning mist.
When you walk down Fifth Avenue in your lavender suit,
your pony eyes opaque, I am the man
beside you, and life is bright
with the finest and best.

And I have seen,
as you have not, such is your modesty,
men turn to watch your tangle of golden hair,
your graceful carriage and unhurried air
as if you belonged to history
or '*her* story', that mystery.
You might have been

a saint or a great
courtesan, anachronistic now
in some ways, in some ways more up-to-date
than the most advanced of those we know.
While you sit on your sun-porch in Connecticut
re-reading Yeats in a feminist light,
I am there with you.

Pygmalion and Galatea

(Ovid, *Metamorphoses*, X, 245-277)

Pygmalion lived for years alone
without a wife to call his own.
Meanwhile, ingeniously, he wrought
a maiden out of ivory, one
lovelier than any woman born,
and with this shape he fell in love.
Alive, she seemed, and apt to move
if modesty did not prevent —
so did his art conceal his art.
He gazed at her in wonderment
and felt her limbs to be quite sure
that she was ivory, nothing more.
Her 'skin' responded to his stroke
or so he thought; and so he spoke,
seized her, imagining his thick
fingers sank into her back,
and looked for bruises on the work.
He whispered gentle, loving words,
brought presents, shells and pebbles, birds
and flowers, things that please young girls;
he clothed her, putting diamond rings
on her white fingers, ropes of pearls
about her neck and breasts. These things
were gorgeous, certainly, although
the naked sculpture even more so.
He laid her down on a bed spread
with sheets dyed a Tyrian red,
called her his lover, propped her head
among soft, feathery pillows as if
a statue might have sensuous life.
   Now Venus' feast-day was the date
and Cyprus thronged to celebrate.
Heifers, their spread horns freshly gilt,

9

had felt the death-stroke to the hilt
in their soft necks, as white as snow,
and the air smoked with incense. Now
Pygmalion, having devoutly laid
gifts on the altar, shyly prayed:
'Gods, if it's true that you can give
anything, grant I may make love — '
Too shy to say 'the maid', he said,
' — to someone *like* my ivory maid!'
But Venus, there in person, knew
what he intended and, to show
that she approved, the altar flames
shot up into the air three times.
Hastening home, the impatient lover
ran to the maid and, leaning over,
embraced her there on her chaste couch.
Her skin seemed warmer to his touch;
his fingers felt her thighs, at which
the ivory grew soft between
his thumbs, as wax melts in the sun
and, gently worked by loving hands,
stretches, relaxes and expands,
responsive even as it responds.
    He stood amazed, still doubtful, thought
himself mistaken, and then not;
inflamed, he stroked her thighs again
until the statue blushed! Each vein
fluttered as our protagonist,
pouring out thanks to Venus, thrust
his lips upon live lips at last.
The maid, feeling his kisses, raised
shy eyes to the sun and, in a glance,
saw daylight and his face at once.
The goddess, with her genial presence,
sanctioned the union and in time

a girl, Paphos, was born to them —
from whom the city takes its name.

An Orphan at the Door

from the Irish of Nuala Ní Dhomhnaill

As fragile as a shell
cast up on a rocky shore,
I stand outside your door
in the afternoon. The bell
rings deep in your house,
echoing in the long, empty rooms.

The kitchen radio howls
rock music and, for a moment,
I feel a surge of hope before
I realize it's only there
to deter thieves, and a long
wait lies before me
with no sound of your step.

I ring again and the echo rises
among high ceilings, wooden stairs.
Peering through the letter-box
I recognize in the Georgian proportions
an intricate crystal structure
that bodies forth and hides a god.

A red rose stands in a vase
on the hall table; a sweater
hangs from the banister;
unopened letters lie about
carelessly on the floor;
but nowhere is there a sign
of you to be seen.

Over the drawing-room fireplace
a postcard from your lover
boasts that hers is the first

mail in your new house. It shows
a simple tourist view
of the tumulus at Newgrange.

There is a reference — not lost
on you, of course —
to the *hieros gamos*, the marriage
made in heaven. Outside
the warm conspiracy of your love
I stand, a nobody,
an orphan at the door.

An icy wind blows through the cold porches
of the farthest pavilions
in the depths of my soul;
the rivers of emotion are frozen solid;
my heart beats wildly
like strange and treacherous seas.

Damn my wooden head, my feather brain,
why am I waiting here
at your closed door?
When the bell peals inside
like the Angelus, do I really
expect the sky to open and a dove
to descend upon me from above?

It's only in the soul
that the miracles take place
of love, forgiveness and grace;
it's only in dream-truth
that the sun and moon shine
together in a bright sky
while day dawns on them both.

The Travel Section

after Laforgue

I'm reading about life on the prairie and frontier
when my heart cries: 'Hey, you could live here!'
Outcast from the old world, a 'desperado'
without God or governance, where could I not go?
Out there I'll scalp my European brain,
run wild like a young colt on the open plain —
a sort of post-literate, Huck Finn child of nature
or existential citizen of the future,
an idealistic rustic, rancher, architect,
hunter, fisherman, gambler, above party and sect;
and live, buckskin-clad, on rye whiskey and pot-roast
between Colorado and the Pacific Coast,
sleeping out under pre-Columbian skies
more generous than our bourgeois certainties!
And? A mystique of camp-sites, the 'Lynch' law,
rough diamonds to clutch in my grubby paw,
a gold-rush over the desert at first light,
a poker school around the fire at night . . .
When I grow old, a farm in the sunrise,
a dairy cow, grandchildren at my knees,
and on the horned gates wrought with my own skill
a split-pine sign-board reading: 'Lazy L'.
And if fond memories of the Place Vendôme
or the high hopes of my contemporaries
should tempt me into thoughts of going home
or the rocky buzzard come to symbolize
the infinite, as opposed to the purple sage,
I'll start a new cult of the Golden Age
with its own code based on holistic books,
blithe and post-modern, for the post-pastoral folks.

THE HUDSON LETTER

for Patricia King

Thou wast not born for death, immortal Bird!
No hungry generations tread thee down;
The voice I hear this passing night was heard
In ancient days by emperor and clown:
Perhaps the self-same song that found a path
Through the sad heart of Ruth when, sick for home,
She stood in tears amid the alien corn;
The same that oft-times hath
Charm'd magic casements, opening on the foam
Of perilous seas, in faery lands forlorn.
     — John Keats, 'Ode to a Nightingale'

Left completely to his own devices, the bachelor's idea of
interior decoration is a pyramid of empty beer-cans on a
window-sill.
     — P. J. O'Rourke, *The Bachelor Home Companion*

I do hate people who come knocking late.
     — Eartha Kitt

I

Sometimes, from beyond the skyscrapers, the cry of a
tug-boat finds you in your insomnia, and you remember
this desert of iron and cement is an island.
                    — Albert Camus, *American Journals,*
                                      tr. Hugh Levick

Winter; a short walk from the 10th St. Pier —
and what of the kick-start that should be here?
The fishy ice lies thick on Gansevoort
around the corner, and the snow shines bright
about your country house this morning: short
the time left to find the serenity
which for a lifetime has eluded me . . .
A rented 'studio apartment' in New York
five blocks from the river, time to think and work,
long-suffering friends and visitors, the bars
where Dylan Thomas spent his final hours,
God rest him; but there's something missing here
in this autistic slammer, some restorative
laid like a magic wand on everything —
on bed, chair, desk and air-conditioner.
Oh, show me how to recover my lost nerve!
The radiators knock, whistle and sing.
I toss and turn and listen, when I wake,
to the first bird and the first garbage truck,
hearing the 'lordly' Hudson 'hardly' flow
to New York Harbour and the sea below.
The lights go out along the Jersey shore
and, as Manhattan faces east once more,
dawn's early light on bridge and water-tower,
Respighi's temperate nightingale on WQXR
pipes up though stronger stations throng the air,
a radio serendipity to illustrate
the resilience of our lyric appetite,
carnivalesque or studiously apart —

on tap in offices, lofts and desperate 'hoods
to Lorca's 'urinating multitudes'
while I make coffee and listen for the news
at eight; but first the nightingale. Sing, Muse.

11 *Last Night*

Here I was, sitting quietly in my 'studio'
and grading papers with the radio low
as Pascal says we should, when out of the blue,
'out there', under the fire-escape, some psycho
sends up a stream of picturesque abuse
directed, evidently, at my 4th-floor window,
his reasoning trenchant, complex and abstruse —
one of those paranoids who seem to know
the system's out to get them even so;
for paranoia, of course, is no excuse.
A nervous terrier, left home alone
and maddened, maybe, by the relentless tone,
went crazy, hollering in the flat below;
then it was time for the lunatic upstairs
to shift his desk and re-align his chairs,
a *West Side Story* love-scene on the sidewalk,
whoop of police sirens, car-alarms
unanimous as in a California 'quake
while some lay dreaming in each others' arms.
Around five a hand, with Gershwin nonchalance,
shook up the empties in the recycling bin
at the corner, shivering for a drop of gin,
its movements brisk, fastidious and, all at once,
successful . . . Dawn; the kick-start as some heroine
draws on her gloves for the Harley-Davidson dream trip
to Provincetown, Key West or Sunset Strip.
Tired vents exhale; cloudy windows condense;
vague vapours pearl fire hydrant and chain-link fence;
and the homeless gaze with satire or indifference
from cardboard boxes on a 'commercial site'
as she sets out on her epic expedition.
To each his haste, to each his dreamt occasion.
Nor snow, nor rain, nor sleet, nor gloom of night
stays these swift couriers from their appointed flight.

iii *Global Village*

The reader need only . . . separate in his own thoughts
the being of a sensible thing from its being perceived.
— George Berkeley,
The Principles of Human Knowledge

This morning, from beyond abandoned piers
where the great liners docked in former years,
a fog-horn echoes in deserted sheds
known to Hart Crane, and in our vigilant beds.
No liners now, nothing but ice and sleet,
a late flame flickering on Brodsky St.
News-time in the global village — Bosnia, famine, drought,
whole nations, races, evicted even yet,
rape victim and blind beggar at the gate —
the images forming which will be screened tonight
on CNN and *The McNeil-Lehrer News Hour*,
the sense of being right there on the spot
— a sense I get right here that Gansevoort
has no 'existence, natural or real, apart
from its being perceived by the understanding'. Not
that I seriously doubt the reality of the Hudson Bar
and Diner; but the skills of Venturi, Thompson, Rowse
that can make post-modern a 19th-century warehouse
and those of Hollywood *film noir* have combined
to create virtual realities in the mind
so the real thing tells us what we already know:
American Gothic. Obviously I don't mean
to pen yet one more craven European
paean to the States, nor would you expect me to,
not being a yuppie in a pinstripe suit
but an Irish Bohemian even as you are too
though far from the original 'Ballroom of Romance',
far too from your posh convent school in France.
Out here, in the clear existential light,
I miss the half-tones I'm accustomed to:

an amateur immigrant, sure I like the corny
humanism and car-stickers — 'I ♥ NY' —
and yet remain sardonic and un-*chic*,
an undesirable 'resident alien' on this shore,
a face in the crowd in this 'off-shore boutique'
inscribed with the ubiquitous comic-strip blob-speak
— LOVE ONE ANOTHER, RESIST INSIPID RHYME —
exposed in thunderstorms, as once before,
and hoping to draw some voltage one more time
or at least not die of spiritual cowardice.
'After so many deaths I live and write'
cried, once, Geo. Herbert in his Wiltshire plot:
does lightning ever strike in the same place twice?

IV Waterfront

We shall go down like palaeolithic man
Before some new Ice Age or Genghiz Khan.
                    — Louis MacNeice,
                    'An Eclogue for Christmas'

Chaste convalescents from an exigent world,
we come to rivers when we are young or old;
stir-crazy, driven by cabin fever, I choose
the 10th St. Pier and toddle into the cold.
Where once the waters spun to your fierce screws
— *Nieuw Amsterdam, Caronia, Île de France!* —
ice inches seaward in a formal dance
where now, adrift with trash and refuse barges,
the photo-realist estuary 'discharges
its footage' into the blind Atlantic snow.
Smoky and crepitant, glacier-spiky, rough
in its white logic, it is a lithograph
from *The Ancient Mariner*, from *Scott's Last Voyage*
or *The Narrative of Arthur Gordon Poe*;
and old Heraclitus might have walked here too
where ice confines the crippled QE2.
This morning, though, the throes of a warm snap
so ice cracks far off like a thunderclap
somewhere along Bohemia's desert coast
and puffs drift in the harsh riparian light,
gun-cotton against storm-clouds in the west
that rain infection and industrial waste,
though now we emerge from the industrial night;
and I recall my ten-year-old delight
at the launch of a P & O liner in Belfast,
all howling 'O God Our Help in Ages Past',
tugs hooting, loose tons of chain rattling into the tide.
I hear no Jersey blackbird serenade
this rapt friar on the Big Apple side;
yet, having come so far from home,

I try to imagine our millennium
where, in the thaw-water of an oil-drum,
the hot genes of the future seethe. The sun
shines on the dump, not on the *côte d'azur*
and not on the cloistered murals, to be sure.
— QUESTION REALITY. DEATH IS BACK. MIGUEL 141.

v 'To Mrs. Moore at Inishannon'

*The statue's sculptor, Frédéric-Auguste Bartholdi, reacted
with horror to the prospect of immigrants landing near
his masterpiece; he called it 'a monstrous plan'. So much
for Emma Lazarus . . . I wanted to do homage to the
ghosts.*
— Mary Gordon, *Good Boys and Dead Girls*

No. 1, Fifth Avenue, New York City, Sept. 14th, 1895
— and Mother, dear, I'm glad to be alive
after a whole week on the crowded *Oceanic* —
tho' I got here all right without being sick.
We boarded in the rain, St. Colman's spire
shrinking ashore, a few lamps glimm'ring there
(*'Will the last to leave please put out the lights?'*),
and slept behind the engines for six nights.
A big gull sat at the masthead all the way
from Roche's Point to Montock, till one day
it stagger'd up and vanish'd with the breeze
in the mass'd rigging by the Hudson quays . . .
Downtown, dear God, is like a glimpse of Hell
in a 'hot wave': drunken men, the roaring 'El',
the noise and squalour indescribable.
(Manners are rough and speech indelicate;
more teeming shore than you cd. shake a stick at.)
However, the Kellys' guest-house; church and tram;
now, thanks to Mrs. O'Brien, here I am
at last, install'd amid the kitchenware
in a fine house a short step from Washington Square.
Protestants, mind you, and a bit serious
much like the Bandon sort, not fun like us,
the older children too big for their britches
tho' Sam, the 4-yr.-old, has me in stitches:
in any case, the whole country's under age.
I get each Sunday off and use the privilege
to explore Broadway, the new Brooklyn Bridge

or the Statue of Liberty, copper torch on top
which, wd. you believe it, actually lights up,
and look at the Jersey shore-line, blue and gold:
it's all fire and sunlight here in the New World.
Eagles and bugles! Curious their simple faith
that stars and stripes are all of life and death —
as if Earth's centre lay in Central Park
when we both know it runs thro' Co. Cork.
Sometimes at night, in my imagination,
I hear you calling me across the ocean;
but the money's good, tho' I've had to buy new clothes
for the equatorial climate. I enclose
ten dollars, more to come (here, for God's sake,
they fling the stuff around like snuff at a wake).
'Bye now; and Mother, dear, you may be sure
I remain
      yr. loving daughter,
              — Bridget Moore.

VI

*Je n'ai pu percer sans frémir ces portes d'ivoire ou de
corne qui nous séparent du monde invisible.*
— Gérard de Nerval,
preface to *Les Chimères*

INSIDER TRADING REPORTS ARE LINKED TO PRICE OF BONDS
NO SOLUTION AT HAND WHILE NUCLEAR WASTE PILES UP
NEW YORK TOUGHING IT OUT TO GET THROUGH THE COLD
ALT SEX MF FF NIGHT OWL SCAT PEDO SNUFF
AT&T BOEING CHRYSLER DUPONT DIGITAL DOW JONES
EXXON GENERAL MOTORS IBM NYNEX SEARS
PARANOIA WEST SIDE ROMEOS AMERICA AFTER DARK
ESCAPED BRONX SEABIRDS SPOTTED IN CENTRAL PARK . . .
. . . On ledge and rail they sit, Inca tern and Andean gull, who
fled their storm-wrecked cage in the Bronx Zoo
and now flap in exhilaration and growing fear
above Yonkers, New Rochelle, Great Neck, Elmhurst,
    Astoria,
Long Beach, Red Hook, Bay Ridge, the whole 'tri-state area',
a transmigration of souls, crazy-eyed as they peer
through mutant cloud-cover and air thick with snow-dust,
toxic aerosol dazzle and invasive car-exhaust,
or perch forlorn on gargoyle and asbestos roof,
fine-featured, ruffled, attentive, almost too high to hear
the plaintive, desolate cab-horns on Madison and Fifth:
like Daisy's Cunard nightingale, they belong in another life.
They are intrigued, baffled and finally bored stiff
by the wised-up Mondrian millions lunching far below
but vulnerable too as, askance, they stare
at the alien corn of Radio City, Broadway and Times Square
and up again at the clouds: where on earth can they go?
'They won't touch garbage'; so where and what will they eat?
If you see one of these nervous birds on ledge or sill
(dark blue, light grey, white head and tail, red bill),
contact the Manhattan Avian Rehab Centre

28

— (212) 689-3039 — and ask for Clare or Jill;
though, to be frank, their chances are less than fair
nor, to be honest, is our confidence great
that these rare species will be fit to compete
in the fight for survival on the city street
with urban gulls, crows, and other toughs of the air.

VII *Sneakers'*

*It's the last harbour. No-one here has to worry about
where they're going next, because there's no farther
they can go.*
— Eugene O'Neill,
The Iceman Cometh

*There is no question there is an unseen world: the
question is, how far is it from mid-town and how late is
it open?*
— Woody Allen

I have drunk, and seen the spider.
— *The Winter's Tale*,
Act II, sc. 1.

'Shut that fuckin' door!' 'Shit, man.' 'Colorado.'
'Hey, Joe! — Another Gibson, Scotch on the rocks
and a mineral water for our friend.' 'No shit.'
'Myself, I've never been the marrying kind.'
'The smartest men in the States.' 'Get outa here.'
'That's 26 for Wake Forest, 18 for Notre Dame;
Durcan replaces Heaney.' 'Don't pay no union dues.'
'. . . got outa jail, cleaned up a little.' 'Just do it.'
'Enough already.' 'Deal with it.' 'Get a life.'
'Think about it.' 'Just another girl on the IRT.'
  I've been a sinner, I've been a scamp
  But now I'm willing to trim my lamp.
'No shit.' 'They broke her up at the end of the war
and sold her cocktail bar to a hotel.'
'I'm kinda queer for girls.' 'Get outa here.'
'Shut that fuckin' door.' 'Have yiz no homes to go to?'
'I've been thrown outa better places than this.'
  But now that I have seen the light
  I'm good by day and I'm good by night.
'You get warm and dry, *tsunami* and tornadoes,

the trade winds move the surface water, right?'
'Peruvian currents.' 'Droughts in Indonesia.'
'You see the fuckin' dikes are crackin' up in Europe?'
'Cyclone.' 'Bermuda Triangle.' 'Black hole.'
'Cutty Sark on the racks and change for the machine.'
'When the guys who tested positive started
biting people, I thought, I'm outa here.'
'Shit, man.' 'No shit.' 'Git ouda here.'
'I sailed with the Blue Star to Buenos Aires,
Shanghai, Tahiti . . . ' 'Git adda here, the Blue Star
never went to Tahiti.' 'Sure did.' 'You better believe it.'
'Don't become a statistic.' 'I'm stupid, I can't help it.'
'Do you want to be patronized by those sons of bitches?'
   I want to join your happy band
   And play all day in the promised land.
'One dollar to Staten Island, fifty cents to Hoboken.'
'Shut that fuckin' door!' 'No shit.' 'Giddaddaheah.'
'Giddout your swimsuits, girls, the ice's broken!'

VIII

(Ovid, *Met.*, VI, 647-674)

Women are necessarily capable of almost anything in
their struggle for survival and can scarcely be convicted
of such man-made crimes as 'cruelty'.
                                                    — F. Scott Fitzgerald,
                                                    Tender is the Night

When his wronged wife Procne sat him down to eat
King Tereus little knew what was on his plate.
(Afternoon now, some silence in the street
till released children dash to bus and swing.)
Pretending this dinner was a traditional thing,
an Athenian feast fit only for a king,
she excused the servants. Throned in his royal seat,
poor Tereus sipped his wine in solitary state
and, carving his own son hot from a covered dish,
called out: 'Hey, send young Itys here to me!'
Procne could barely conceal her wicked glee
and, keen to tell him the ghastly news, replied,
pointing at Tereus' stomach: 'There he is inside!'
'What do you mean?' says Tereus, looking foolish,
'I don't see him.' Then, as he called once more,
fair Philomela appeared, dripping with blood, and flung
Itys' severed head, itself streaming with gore,
right in Tereus' face, as he picked at his own young.
Oh, how she longed then for the use of her tongue!
Nothing would have given her greater pleasure
than to say a few harsh words to her ravisher.
As for the Thracian king, he nearly had a seizure
to think that he should eat his . . . own son Itys.
Howling, he swept aside the candlesticks
and called the furies from the depths of Styx;
no, howling he overturned the dinner table
and called the furies from the ~~halls~~ hobs of Hell.

Unhinged to think this flesh of his own flesh
consumed by the viscera where the genes first grew
and he his own son's charnel-house, he drew
his sword to open his own digestive tract
and pluck the chewed-up gobbets from the mush
but turned instead on the two sisters, who fled
as if on wings; and they *were* winged, in fact,
both of them changed in a twinkling into birds
whirring and twittering inches above his head,
swallow and nightingale hovering in mid-air.
One flew to the roof-top, one flew to the woods
where, even today, the nightingale can be heard
descanting in convent garden and Georgian square —
while Tereus, with hair on end and furious sword-bill,
turned into a hoopoe and is furious still . . .
. . . Never mind the hidden agenda, the sub-text;
it's not really about male arrogance, 'rough sex'
or vengeful sisterhood, but about art
and the encoded mysteries of the human heart.

IX

(Rory and Katie)

All you need to do is remember a tune
no-one else has thought of.
                                — attrib. Schubert

'Nature, not having included me in her plan,
has treated me like an uninvited guest'
— Turgenev, *Diary of a Superfluous Man*.
Uneaten, you call home while I take a rest.
It's 9.00 p.m. London time when your mother
picks up the phone 3,000 miles away
in Shepherd's Bush. Dinner is nearly over
perhaps, and the BBC News on the box
(Soviet disintegration, 'Anglo-Irish' talks)
as it used to be, while on the sofa lie
new fiction, Jacobean drama, philosophy,
the *Observer* Magazine and the *Daily Mail*.
— I'm guessing . . . Tell me, son, do you recall,
ten years ago now, when our 'little platoon'
would march round Barrie's pond each sunny Sunday afternoon?
Out here for the World Cup and having a ball,
you talk to your sister now in that lost domain
describing how, holed up in a brownstone
on Morton St., and painting the walls in lieu
of rent, you're goofing off tonight to a party below Canal
with friends in the film scene and the grunge rock milieu;
then on I come ('Hi, Katie!') with (Kavanagh's rhyme) my banal
'Happy Birthday' and 'Happy St. Valentine's Day'
and my lame excuses for not being able to pay
the school fees this time round; and I feel,
all of a sudden, like the worst kind of heel.
Sometimes, as I sit in the Knickerbocker or stand up there
in Columbia University like Philby in Red Square,
I blush like a traitor; but what kind of a traitor?

35

A traitor to the past? To a country not our own?
To the land of fiscal rectitude and spiritual desolation?
The 'family values' brigade? The conservative task-force?
The gene militia? The armies of the unborn?
I know 'our loyalty to unhappiness', of course,
'the feeling that this is where we really belong';
and yet, across 3,000 miles of water
and five time-zones, my own prayer for my daughter
would be, not innocence and ceremony
exactly, but a more complicated grace,
the sort of thing you play on the boxed lyre when you're alone
in the House of Atreus, something slow and meditative,
some rich myth of reconciliation
as if a statue moved and began to live —
for I like to think all this is a winter's tale
around a hearth (but whose?); and that when we tell
the story ten years hence you'll be able to say,
'Thou mettest with things dying, I with things new-born.'
A precocious feminist, already at the age of five
contemptuous of your raggedy dolls, derisive
yet *seerious*, you could say 'paranoia' and the Greek for
     ice-cream
and told a flirtatious Montague not to interrupt your dream;
so I know you'd take a pretty satirical view
of the daft cards and naff hearts in the stores right now
— 'Be Mine', you know what I mean, 'I Dream Only of You' —
yet at American dusk, if I catch, as I sometimes do,
a TV-lighted, nuclear-family glimpse
of pillows, home computers and Noguchi lamps,
the pram in the hall, the table set for tea,
it sets me thinking of old times and how,
too busy growing up myself, I failed to watch you grow.
Some time soon you must visit this musical city
to hear Purcell in Carnegie Hall, an American string quartet,
Eartha Kitt at the St. Regis, *Il Trovatore* at the Met.

I've had neither the authority nor the opportunity
to tell you about the things you need to know,
as your mother will: how not to rely on looks
only, but on acquired skills and the wisdom found in books—
up to a point, of course . . . You were a scream,
therefore a born artist, but even the *being* is an art
we learn for ourselves, in solitude, on our very own,
listening to the innermost silence of the heart,
prolonging the inconsequence of a gaze
and dreaming at all times our uninterruptable dream
of redemptive form. I saw a film recently,
Glenn Gould playing Bach to the Canadian wilderness,
the great chords crashing out into empty space,
the music of planet Earth, the music of a sphere
no-one's remembered in any other place
so far as we know, and thought, the glorious racket
we use to explain ourselves in perpetuity
to our hi-tech geological posterity
at the frozen outer reaches of the galaxy.
It's ridiculous but *just do it*, as they say here;
make noise without embarrassment or fear. Take it
from the top, Katie; yours is the sound we want to hear!

x Auden on St. Mark's Place

If equal affection cannot be,
Let the more loving one be me.

Hail, floppy-slippered bear of St. Mark's Place!
I seem to glimpse your cheesy, limestone face
where you loom at a dirty window, gin in paw,
on a hot evening during the great Cold War.
The young Trotsky wrote and printed *Novy Mir*
in the basement, now a xerox joint; but your
own permanent revolution is the resilient spirit
of the risen Christ, your multicultural heaven
illuminating the new world we inherit,
redeeming by intellectual grace and merit
the *Unaufgeklärten* in the boondocks, even.
Joseph the druggist, Abe in the liquor store,
Maurice the mailman, Elizabeth Mayer and Marianne Moore
are the happier for your grumpy love; for, funny
in Hobbit T-shirt and dubious Levi's, you
were a victim of nothing but irony, Gramsci's new
'disease of the interregnum'; and to castration-
and-death phone-threats replied without hesitation:
'I think you've the wrong number.' Lord of martini
and clerihew, who saw Rome and the other empires
fall, who were so insistent on your privacy,
who so valued personal responsibility,
what would you make now of the retentive *pax*
Americana, our world of internet and fax,
a still-thriving military-industrial complex,
situational ethics, exonerative 12-step programs,
health fascism, critical theory and 'smart' bombs?
While we hole up in our bath-houses and catacombs,
votaries of Eros if not always of Aphrodite,
I see you ride at rush-hour with your rich pity
and self-contempt an uptown train packed to the doors
with 'aristocratic Negro faces', not like ours,

or reciting 'The Unknown Citizen' at the 'Y'.
When will she — Gaia, Clio — send downpours
to silence the 'gnostic chirrup' of her calumniators?
When will we hear once more the pure voice of elation
raised in the nightwood of known symbol and allusion?
Oh, far from Mother, in the unmarried city,
you contemplate a new ode to Euphrosyne,
goddess of banquets; and in the darkest hours
of holocaust and apocalypse, cheap music and singles bars,
you remind us of what the examined life involves —
for what you teach is the courage to be ourselves,
however ridiculous; and if you were often silly
or too 'prone to hold forth', you prescribe a cure
for our civilization and its discontents
based upon *agapé*, Baroque opera, common sense
and the creative impulse that brought us here,
sustaining us now as we face a more boring future.

XI *Chinatown*

Sun's eye at cloud-rift like the ideogram for speakeasy.
                                        — Michael O'Brien,
                                        'Perceptual Difficulties'

the chimera of a dioxide sunset
                                        — Mary O'Donnell,
                        Spiderwoman's Third Avenue Rhapsody

The wind of the common people whirls from lanes and
alleys, poking the rubbish, stirring up the dust . . .
                                        — Hsiang Ch'u, 3rd c.

. . . and whips the pagodas of Confucius Square.
MIGUEL 141. DEATH IS BACK. FIND THE CURE.
A rackety sunset under a storm-lit sky
where we sit, uncool dad and laconic son,
amid the festive clatter of Son Low Kee,
dining on midnight mussels and sesame prawn
torn from the hairy darkness of the sea.
A crackle of firecrackers all over the ward
for the Chinese New Year, Gambino and Genovese
having moved on. 'Where the broom fails to reach,'
said Mao, 'the dust won't clear of its own accord';
but we like it here in this ethnocentric refuge
under the fairy lights of Brooklyn Bridge
where the quiet or chattering families sit at board.
We're one of the quiet tables as we review
your temporary job, tonight's occasion.
You're listening to Guns 'n' Roses, Simple Minds, U2 —
and reading *Moby-Dick*, according to you;
but I recognize your strategies of evasion
for I too was young and morose — worse, sinister — in youth
a frightful little shit, to tell the truth,
a disaffected boy — my face, like Keats',

'pressed to a sweet-shop window' full of treats;
a rancorous paragon of bile and sloth
in the days of nihilism and alienation,
though house-trained by your mother later on:
in any event, those ancient days are gone
like the T'ang Dynasty and the shoes of 1941.
We are all lost boys, or so we like to imagine —
each sprung, like Gatsby, from his own self-conception;
whereas, of course, there's not much you can do
about the odd parents who conceived of you
and being young, I remember it well, is tough:
will the last bus be gone, her light be on or off?
I wouldn't do it again for all the tea in Taiwan;
but, now that you've reached the age of rock and soccer
and I the age of 'serious medicine',
let me, Polonius of the twilight zone
— a pseudo-Dionysus, his oats sown —
offer you some belated, functional succour.
I need hardly speak to you in praise of women
since you grew up amongst them. (So did I
but there's a tale will keep indefinitely.)
Be thou familiar but by no means vulgar; shun
the fatuous rectitude of received opinion,
new-speak and euphemism. Don't 'stick up for your rights'
or worry about your self-esteem; contrive
your own life and live it by your own lights
where such considerations don't apply.
Costly thy habit as thy purse can buy.
Be sceptical but whole-hearted; don't be shy;
avoid spirits and nicotine; read Stendhal on love;
trust your own instincts, even the most fugitive;
and welcome to *la condition humaine*.
Cheer up, son; oh, and above all disbelieve
the cynic who tries to tell you how to behave
for, as Confucius said, fine words are seldom humane.

XII *Alien Nation*

These chronic homeless are mostly single adults who
have given up seeking help because they feel the
'system' has given up on them and is largely unrespon-
sive to their needs. Many are substance abusers . . .
Getting high or drunk may be the only way they know
of alleviating their pain and disappointment.
            — *What You Can Do to Help the Homeless*
                        (Simon and Schuster, 1991)

RX GOTHAM DRUG GAY CRUISES SONY LIQUORS MARLBORO
ADULT VIDEO XXX BELSHAZZAR FIND THE CURE
IGLESIA ADVENTISTA DEL 7MO. DIA . . .
. . . We come upon them in the restless dark
in the moon-shadow of the World Trade Centre
with Liberty's torch glimmering over the water,
glued to a re-run of *The Exterminator*
on a portable TV in a corner of Battery Park
(some have park views, others sleep in the park);
and think how sensible the alternative polity
beneath the ostensible, pharaonic city
glimpsed through rain or dust from an expressway —
the old clothes, packing cases and auto trunks
seen everywhere from here to the South Bronx,
its population growing by the week, by the day,
oblivious to our chaos theories and data banks,
from the Port Authority Bus Terminal to JFK
and farther afield, in freight-yard and loading bay,
gull-screaming landfill, stripped trailer and box-car,
the gap increasing between the penthouse tower
and the desert of cinder-block and razor-wire
watered by truck-stop rainbow and sun-shower,
or behind the Ritz-Carlton and Holiday Inn.
Spare a thought, friend; spare a dime, bud; spare the price of a
    Bud
for the fourth world of Napoleon's 'fifth element', mud.

Poor banished children of Eve (brain damage, delirium,
peripheral neuritis), with nowhere to call home
(*Third box-car midnight train to Bangor, Maine*),
we are all survivors in this rough terrain;
I know you and you me, you wretched buggers,
and I've no problem calling you my brothers
for I too have been homeless and in detox
with baaad niggas 'n' crack hoes on the rocks
and may be there again, for all I know —
who, once a strange child with a taste for vorse,
would lurch at 3.00 a.m. through drifting snow
to the Lion's Head, McKenna's, the White Horse;
but 'even the inert contribute to the universe',
even perceived losers have often won
for there, of course, a different truth is known.
Blown here like particles from an exploding sun,
we are all far from home, be our home still
a Chicago slum, a house under the Cave Hill
or a caravan parked in a field above Cushendun.
Clutching our bits and pieces, arrogant in dereliction,
we are all 'out there', filling the parks and streets
with our harsh demand: 'Sleep faster, we need the sheets!'
An ocean breeze, wild-flower-scented, soft and warm,
blows downtown where we part beneath the moon;
a Haitian driver, riffing like Racine,
whisks me up Hudson St. in a thunderstorm.

XIII *Sappho in 'Judith's Room'*

What is important now is to recover our senses; in place
of a hermeneutics we need an erotics of art.
— Susan Sontag,
Against Interpretation (1964)

The reed-voiced nightingale has been my guide,
soft-spoken announcer of spring, whose song I set
against a cult of contention I decried —
except, of course, for 'the fight to be affectionate'.
A corps of men, a list of ships? Give me instead
my non-violent girls — Cydro, Gongula — and particularly
our glamorous Anactoria somewhere over the sea
whose eyes' mischievous sparkle remains to me
a finer sight than Homeric bronze; for now,
like the moon rising at sunset, casting its glow
on the waves, on evening meadows of brine and dew,
she climbs the night sky, and perhaps her heart too
is heavy with recollection, perhaps out there she hears
the wind among the reeds, and calls, so the soft-petal'd ears
of darkness hear her, and the dividing sea.
Aphrodite, weaver of intrigue, revisit my heart
as so often before in your dove-drawn chariot.
Nothing was alien to me, nothing inhuman:
what did I teach but the love of women?
Soon, when the moon and Pleiades have gone,
in the vast silence of the night I shall lie alone
or sit here, 'tenth Muse', in this American bookstore
relishing the historical ironies in store
and the 'homeless flow of life' beyond the door.
The authors are all women, and I myself
am represented on the poetry shelf
(miraculously, I hold here in my hands
stanzas exhumed from the Egyptian sands);
for if harsh Nature made me short and dark
she picked me out to do immortal work

and grades my stature, slight though I seem to be,
in lines of verse that are still read even here
and not just by my own Sapphic coterie.
Sure I've been down to the dead kingdom to hear
the grim statistics, and seen with my own eyes
women and children in their extremities
— 'cholera, typhus, croup, diphtheria' —
but, beyond speech and the most inclusive song,
my theme is love and love's *daimonic* character,
a site of praise and not of grievances
whatever the torment — which we meet, if wise,
in our best festive and ingenious guise.
Let of old Plato frown the eye austere,
before the *cafeneion* I'd sit when young
in sea-girt Mytilene of the dirty dances
making eye contact with new acquaintances
and relishing our sweet Æolian tongue;
and, now that I exceed in fame our fine
Alcaeus, the laureate of politics and wine
whose high style was more 'serious' than mine,
the bad girls of my cult, an ardent choir
whose shafts shivered their music in my lyre,
votaries of Aphrodite, a nubile crowd,
still gather here to hear me read aloud;
and if I cling still to an old favouritism
or fall for a younger man from time to time
('Men without women grow stupid, women without men pine')
I'm happiest here in a place like Judith's Room
with Djuna, Janis, Gloria, Brooke and Kim.
Girls all, be with me now and keep me warm —
didn't I *say* we'd live again in another form?

xiv *Beauty and the Beast*

'I don't know any stories; none of the lost boys
know any stories.'
'How perfectly awful', said Wendy.

— J. M. Barrie,
Peter Pan

I go nightshopping like Frank O'Hara I go bopping
up Bleecker for juice, croissants, Perrier, ice-cream
and Gitanes *filtre*, pick up the laundry, get back
to five (5!) messages on the answering machine
from Mary K. and Eliza, Louis, Barry and Jack,
and on TV sixty channels of mind-polluting yuck.
Thank God for the VCR. Now at last I can screen
the old movies I haven't seen since I was 'young' —
A Night to Remember, Rear Window, High Noon,
The Man Who Never Was, A King in New York . . .
Tonight, for example, tickled to bits, I stick on
the 'original, uncut' version of *King Kong*:
childish, perhaps, but a cultural critic's dream.
I re-wind, fast-forward, and replay the scene
where Kong instals Fay Wray screaming on the high rock
where he lives, and she's attacked by a gryphon, roc,
velociraptor, hoopoe, some such creation,
a thousand feet above the Indian Ocean,
wherever, and you can see the little freighter
sitting far out there on the sparkling water.
Sensitive Kong doesn't interfere with her sexually
though he does *paw* and sniff his fingers, actually,
eyes bright with curiosity; then the entire cast
come tough-talking through the primaeval rain-forest,
chivalrous Robert Armstrong sets her free
and they run off together down to the shore,
indignant Kong chasing them with a roar
because the poor sap really loves her, do you see —
and how exciting it must have been in the heyday

46

of Prohibition, 40% unemployment and the WPA!
— for that matter, it's still thrilling even today.
I sit here like an old child with a new toy
or a creature from outer space, Saturn perhaps,
inventorying the resources of the planet of the apes
when (look!) the huge gorilla, the size of a fly
('Eighth Wonder of the World', says the publicity),
climbs up, like Batman later, the sheer side of the Empire State,
a black speck outlined against the morning sky
clutching Fay, said Noël Coward, 'like a suppository'.
It's all inconsistent, of course, and disproportionate,
he's too small there and too big on the street, *I know*,
but it makes no difference, it's a magnificent show.
. . . The little bi-planes come gunning for him now
and Kong, by Jove, knocks one of them out of the sky
with a hairy hand. They wear him out, of course,
and he falls to extinction among the crowds below.
And Fay??? She screams but she's safe; it might've been worse.
I breathe again and zap, lord of the universe,
the credits. Semiotician, couch potato,
I've had them all here in my room on video —
Leigh, Grahame, Taylor, Kelly and Monroe;
but why so few poems for the women I know?
Because these things used to be open to innuendo?
Fay, born in Alberta, you were also in *Dirigible*
and 'existed most forcefully when faced with terror'
says *Video Guide* — like most of us, probably. Well,
Kong and I dedicate this one to you, old girl,
wherever you are; pushing 90 and hanging in there,
we want you to know we love you and root for you still.

(for Fay Wray)

xv *Domnei*

Quan totz lo segles brunezis
Delai on ylh es si resplan.
— Marcabru

Now that we all get laid and everyone swings,
who needs the formal continence of *l'amour*
courtois and the hang-ups of a provincial clique
before innocence died at Béziers and Montségur?
Still, in the brisk heart a faint voice will speak,
in a star-lit corner of the soul there sings
to an enclosed loved one the intense troubadour
in his quaint language, and his rondeau rings
resiliently on the vineyards, streams and rock-
strewn hillsides of 12th-century Languedoc;
still in her forest tower under the wide rain
of Poitiers, Limoges, Dordogne or Aquitaine
there sleeps the remote, enfamilied chatelaine,
whether privileged by choice or not remains unclear,
or she herself (Marie de Ventadour,
Iseult de Capio) writes to another man —
while Riquier, Bornheil, Vidal and Uc St.-Cir,
the accomplished amateur and the shivering boy
render, beneath her window, a 'chaste' homage.
The sun goes down beyond the known world's edge
and a crescent moon climbs an incurious sky:
Therefore thy kinsmen are no stop to me.
As to the kind of love we mean, they say,
one must be patient, such is its quality —
nor is there place here for the coward, bluffer
or those rhymers who, mingling lies with truth,
corrupt the wife, the husband and the lover
by hinting love adopts a lateral motion,
unsettling merit and estranging youth
so men are jealous, women in confusion.
Perhaps all this was a deplorable thing,

a vicious fiction or a coercive myth;
'but when the earth renews itself in spring
and whitethorn flowers to hear the blackbird sing
I too sing, although she whom I admire
finds little to her taste in what I write.
I praise not only her clear skin and fine eyes
but also her frank speech and distinguished air;
so dumbstruck am I on her visiting days
I can find no words to speak of my desire
yet, when she leaves me, my composure flees.
No-one I know can hold a candle to her
and when the world dims, as it does tonight,
I see the house she goes to blaze with light.'

XVI *Key West*

our little wooden northern houses
                                    — Elizabeth Bishop

Somewhere along Route 1 — Plantation, Tavernier —
cloud-splitting Angie broke over the Keys last year
in June, the earliest ever, bringing torrential rains,
though it wasn't one of those really *terrible* hurricanes
you hear about, that wreck 'homes' and wreak atrocities
on isolated farms, snug harbours, close communities,
but a swift cloud-stream of premonitory showers
that waltzed off, 'mad lutanist', in the direction of New Orleans
irrigating pine and cedar, lemon groves and sand-bars
while the 'still-vex'd' Bahamas heaved in still-turbulent seas.
The outskirts of Key West, when we got there,
you driving, a white bandana round your hair
and Satchmo's 'Wonderful World' on the car radio,
were still where they were supposed to be, and calm
between downpours red poinciana, jasmine, 'royal' palm
and the white frame-houses built a century ago
by tough skippers against cyclone and tornado
whistling in off the Gulf of Mexico.
The town gasped in a tropical heat-wave
and I recalled old Mr. Temple's narrative
in *Key Largo*, the great nameless storm of 1935
that killed 800 people (it did too) and blew
the East Coast Railroad into the ocean — true,
the bridges are still standing, but that was the last train.
Suave, mari magno turbulantis aequora ventis,
e terra magnum alterius spectare laborem:
it's cool, when gale-force winds trouble the waters,
to watch from shore the tribulations of others!
. . . Uh-oh, before dawn it came around again,
fat drops hitting on storm lanterns, demented budgies
screeching beyond the pool and the churning trees;
and I pictured the vast turmoil undersea,

a mute universe of sponge and anemone,
of conch and snapper, octopus and algae,
odd fish of every stripe in their coral conservatories,
while counting the stiff electric chimes of St. Mary's,
    Star of the Sea.
Later, exhausted hens on the telephone lines,
disheveled dogs in the flooded Bahamian lanes:
chaos, *triste tropique* — till, mauve and rose,
flecked with pistachio cloud, a new kind of day arose
and I saw why once to these shores came *other* cold
solitaries down from the north in search of love and poetry
— the mad sailor, the stuffed bullfinch blue and gold,
the shy perfectionist with her painter's eye —
to sing in the crashing, galaxy-lit sea-porches.
It was one of those far-out, raw mornings, the beaches
littered with dreck, and a derelict dawn moon,
mountains and craters in visible cameo, yearned
close to the Earth as if murmuring to return,
milk of what heavenly breast, dew drenching the skin —
a wreckers' morning, with everyone a bit lost
as if landed from Senegal or the Ivory Coast.
Why so soon in the season? Newspapers and TV
spoke of 'El Niño', the fabulous, hot tide-thrust
born in December off Peru like the infant Christ
sea-changing *all* with its rough magic; and advised
of hurricanes to come, so that one feared not only
for the Cuban cabin and the gimcrack condominium
but for the 'sleek and effortless vacation home'
featured in the current issue of *Key Design*,
the 'storm-resistant' dream house with its 'vinyl membrane',
a bait-fridge and 'teak sailfish-fighting chair';
for roads and bridges, lighthouses, any structure
presumed permanent; towns and cities everywhere
vulnerable to a trickle of sand, to a breath of fresh air;
and thought of the fragility of all architecture,

the provisional nature even of aerospace.
I keep on my desk here a coarse handful of Florida sea-moss
and remember, this wintry night, that summery place —
how we strolled out there on the still-quaking docks
shaken but exhilarated, turned to retrace
our steps up Caroline St., and sat in Pepe's
drinking (rum and) Coke with retired hippies
who long ago gave up on the land and settled among the rocks.

XVII *Imbolc: JBY*

*There is something vulgar in all success; the greatest
men fail, or seem to have failed.*
— Oscar Wilde

*The Good has nothing to do with purpose, indeed it
excludes the idea of purpose . . . The only genuine way
to be good is to be good 'for nothing'.*
— Iris Murdoch,
The Sovereignty of Good

A roof over my head, protected from the rain,
I'm reading, 'pilgrim father', your letters to your son
and wondering if, unlike you, I should head for home.
Escaping the turbulence of this modern Rome
in a flurry of skyline views and exploding foam,
I can see that 747 in flight over Nova Scotia,
over Shannon and Limerick, snoring back to the fuchsia,
to that land of the still-real I left in '91,
of Jennifer Johnston and Seosaimhín Ní Gabhráin;
I can see a united Ireland from the air,
its meteorological gaiety and despair,
some evidence of light industry and agriculture,
familiar contours, turf-smoke on field and town;
I can even hear the cabin crew's soft *'fáilte'*
and the strains of 'My Lagan Love' as we touch down.
A recovering Ulster Protestant like you from Co. Down,
I shall walk the Dublin lanes as the days grow shorter,
I who once had a poem in *The New Yorker*,
and spend old age, if any, in an old mac
with the young audibly sneering behind my back,
deafened by gulls and the heart-breaking cries
of children — ourselves, once — by perilous seas
where nightingale never yet dared raise its voice.
Now, listening to the *rus-in-urbe*, spring-in-winter noise
of late-night diners, while the temperatures rise

and the terrible wind-chill factor abates, I realize
the daffodils must be out in ditch and glen
and windows soon flung wide to familiar rain;
and marvel how, a figure out of the past,
'an old man in a hurry', you stuck it here to the last,
the rightful Duke of Ormonde housed like Willie's Bedouin
with only 'an iron bedstead, an old rug' and, of course,
your easel getting the pale north-light, while you
for whom art was never prey to commercial rage
nor beauty sacrificed to a ruthless mortgage
read Shakespeare, Keats and the Russian novelists
(dachas, troika troilism, the endless versts . . .),
negotiating the ice-fields of Eighth Avenue
on your way home past the Blarney Stone and the White Rose,
to die on West 29th of the Asian 'flu —
leaving us, since you never *could* 'do hands',
your unfinished self-portrait just as it stands,
'more sketch than picture' (nothing is ever 'done').
. . . But first you met by chance at the riverside
a young woman with a sick child she tried to hide
(not out of shame, you felt, but anguished pride),
soft-spoken, 'from Donnybrook', amid the alien corn.
'It pained me that her bright image should fade.'
Thus your epiphany, and you wrote to explain:
'The nightingale sings with its breast against a thorn,
it's out of pain that personality is born'
(same thing for the sedge-warbler and the yellow bittern);
and, knowing that we must suffer to be wise
unless, 'like Raphael', we avert our eyes
from a dying infant or an unhappy wife,
you recommended 'the poetry of life'.
Things you understood: children, the human face,
'something finer than honesty', the loneliness
of beautiful women, the priority of the real.
Things that puzzled you: economy, fear,

the argument from design, the need to feel secure,
the belief in another world besides this one here.
Despite your rationalism, did it ever occur
(the obvious next step for a quixotic who
preferred the Virgin to the Dynamo)
that the universe might be *really* 'magical', sir,
and you yourself a showing-forth of that soul?
'Art is dreamland.' When you rejoined the whole
under most of the same stars, and closed your voyage
in a woman friend's family vault beside Lake George,
what glimpse was given to you in the black hole?
Now, to 'Yeats, Artist and Writer', may we add
that you were at home here and in human nature?
— But also, in your own words, lived and died
like all of us, then as now, 'an exile and a stranger'?

XVIII *The Small Rain*

Home lies ahead, in the unfolding of the story in the
future — not behind, waiting to be regained.
                                    — Marina Warner,
                                Six Myths of Our Time

Once upon a time it was let me out and let me go —
the night flight over deserts, amid cloud,
a dream of discipline and fit solitude.
Now, drifters, loners, harsh and disconsolate,
'inane and unappeased', we come knocking late;
and now it's take me back and take me in.
So take us in where we set out long ago,
the secret garden in the lost domain,
the vigilant lamplight glimpsed through teeming rain,
the house, the stove in the kitchen, the warm bed,
the hearth, *vrai lieu*, ranged crockery overhead —
'felicitous space' lost to the tribes. I lodge
one window slightly open to let in the night air
— 10° below, these nights, on average —
thus 'heating the street', the clouds, the stratosphere,
and peer down through the fire-escape. It's broad
day all night on the 24-hr. film-set,
kliegs bright on stadium and construction site;
but a civilization based on superfluous light
concedes no decent dark, so we create
with blinds and blankets our own private night
to keep the glare out. Searchlights and dead stars
pick out the Trump Tower and the United Nations,
the marble halls of finance, the subway walls of the brain,
the good, the bad, the ugly and the insane,
the docks and Governor's Island; and the bars
where the lost and the disappointed feel no pain
are empty except for the all-night populations
with no homes to go to but their eternal one.
This is the hour of the locked door and the shut gate,

harsh blues of the rowdy and the unfortunate,
wolf-howl of the dispossessed, the outcast and the alone:
Hey, man, they got us niggas by the nuts,
Gotta get with the program move our butts.
— Heart murmur, insomnia, liberal conscience, night moans,
forensic fears; pipes knock, a tug-boat groans.
I keep on rappin' till the break of dawn
Although I cannot call my soul my own.
. . . The objects too are conscious in their places —
lamp, chair, desk, oil-heater and bookcases
brisk with a bristling, mute facticity
connecting them to the greater community
of wood and minerals throughout the city.
When the present occupant is no longer here
and durables prove transient, as they do,
all will survive somehow; the pictures too,
prints, posters, reproductions, such as they are:
Botticelli's sea-born, shell-borne Aphrodite,
Dunluce, 'The Doors of Dublin', Whitman in a suit,
Monet skiffs on the Seine, a window by Bonnard,
Leech's convent garden, a Hopper light,
Hokusai's wave, Lichtenstein's *ingénue*
shedding a tear ('B . . . but, Jeff . . . ') beside the door
and (look!) my favourite, over there on the right,
picked up at a yard-sale in Connecticut,
unsigned, 'printed in Sweden', a Munch-like study of two
turn-of-the-century women on a hazy shore,
their intent heads, earnest attitudes and white
clothes bespeaking idealism and questions of the heart,
their footprints in the sand to the waterline,
the human presence since we live here too —
all primal images in their different ways
watching for spring-time and the lengthening days.
Jequirity, monkshood, nightshade, celandine:
the friends and contemporaries begin to go

— Nina Gilliam, Eugene Lambe, and others too.
Now more than ever seems it rich to die
into an oceanic, a molecular sky . . .
'A dry soul is best'; and at night to lie
empty of mind, heart hammering; *and thou,*
great mother, cave of wonders, open now
to our languor the interior of the rose
that closes round ambition, and disclose
your secret, be it Byzantium or the sphere
all centre, no circumference . . . I pretend
you're here beside me; guardian angel, best friend,
practitioner of tough love and conservation,
I'd say make all safe and harmonious in the end
did I not know the voyage is never done
for, even as we speak, somewhere a plane
gains altitude in the moon's exilic glare
or a car slips into gear in a silent lane . . .
I think of the homeless, no rm. at the inn;
far off, the gaseous planets where they spin,
the star-lit towers of Nineveh and Babylon,
the secret voice of nightingale and dolphin,
fish crowding the Verrazano Bridge; and see,
even in the icy heart of February,
primrose and gentian. When does the thaw begin?
We have been too long in the cold. — Take us in; take us in!

— *New York, Dublin,*
January-September, 1995

Acknowledgements

Acknowledgements are due to the editors of *Poetry Ireland Review, The London Review of Books, The New Yorker, American Poetry Review, Poetry* (Chicago) and *The Southern Review* (Louisiana State University), where some of these poems first appeared; to Faber & Faber (London) and Farrar, Straus & Giroux (New York), the publishers of *After Ovid*, ed. Michael Hofmann and James Lasdun; and to the Lannan and Guggenheim Foundations. 'An Orphan at the Door' appeared in *Pharaoh's Daughter* (The Gallery Press/Wake Forest University Press).